365 WRITING PROMPTS FOR KIDS

© Thomas Media

Founded in 2017, Thomas Media is a publisher of gift books, creative books, innovative journals, cards, notepads and stationery. Thomas Media publishes over 50 books and ancillary products per year.

© Thomas Media
Visit us at Thomasmedia.ie

ISBN: 978-1-9998747-3-5
Printed: United States

amazon.com

As a small company, we rely on your reviews to keep costs low for our customers and improve our products. Please spare a moment rate or review this book on Amazon and share your experience with the Amazon community.

All I want for Christmas is...

Last night I dreamed...

If I could go anywhere for vacation I would go...

If you could meet one person from history, who would you choose and why?

What is your favorite day of the week? Why?

What is your favorite sport? Why?

When I got home from school, my parents were not home!
Where were they?

If I were to write a movie, it would be about...

What is your favorite color? Why?

What is your favorite holiday? Why?

What is your favorite animal? Why?

BASIC GRAMMAR RULES

1. Use Active Voice

Everyhumanlanguagestartsanactivesentencewiththesubject,orthe"doer." InEnglish,theverb(what`sbeingdone)followsthesubject.Ifthereisanobject (thereceiveroftheaction),itcomesaftertheverb.Theformulalookslikethis:

S+V+O. This rule is the foundation of the English language.

- Here are some examples:
- Paul walked the dog.
- The dog liked Paul.
- I did not like the dog.

2. Link Ideas with a Conjunction

SometimesyouwanttolinktwoideaswithasecondS+V+Ocombination.When youdo,youneedacoordinatingconjunction.Thenewformulalookslikethis:

S+V+O, COORDINATING CONJUNCTION+S+V+O
Coordinatingconjunctionsareeasytorememberwithanacronimicmnemonic device:

FANBOYS
For | And | Nor | But | Or | Yet | So

3. Use a Comma to Connect Two Ideas As One

FANBOYSareusedwhenconnectingtwoideasasoneinasinglesentence,but don`t forget the comma.

For example:

- I do not walk Paul`s dog, nor do I wash her.
- Paul fed his dog, and I drank coffee.
- Paul feeds and walks his dog every day, but the dog is still wild.

4. Use a Serial Comma in a List

Theserial,orOxford,commaisacontroversialruleofgrammar.Somewantto eliminateitaltogetherwhileothersjustdon`tknowhowtouseit.Theserial commaisthelastcommainalist,usuallyappearingbefore"and."Theserial comma comes after "cat" in this sentence:

- Paul has a dogs, cats, and horses.

Commasseparateunitsinalist.Intheabovecase,eachunitonlyhasonepart, soit`seasy.Wherepeoplegetconfusediswhentheunitsarebigger,buttherule still applies:

- Paul has a dogs, cats, and horses and ponies.

Notice that the serial comma comes before "and" but
not the last "and" in the sentence. The "and" that
follows the comma is only there because it sounds better.
Grammatically, "and" is irrelevant.
Only units matter.

BASIC GRAMMAR RULES

5. Use the Semicolon to Join Two Ideas

Alistofgrammarruleshastoincludethescariestofpunctuationmarks.Itmight lookfunny,butdon`tbeafraidofthesemicolon;it`stheeasiestthingintheworld touse!Sayyouwanttojointwoideasbutcan`tfigureoutorcan`tbebotheredto useacoordinatingconjunction.Thetwoideascanbeseparatesentences,butyou think that they are so closely connected; they really should be one. Use a semicolon.

- Pauls`s dog is hyper; it won`t stop barking or sit still.
- My heart is like a river; it`s bitter and cold.
- Paulhastowalkhisdogeveryday;itisthemostrestlessdoganyonehas ever witnessed.

6. Use the Simple Present Tense for Habitual Actions

Thesimplepresentisthetenseyouuseforanyhabitualaction.Thethingsyou alwaysdoordoeveryTuesdayaredescribedwiththesimplepresent,whichjust means you pick the first form of any verb.

- Paul likes dogs.
- I don`t walk Paul`s dog.
- Paul and I drink coffee every Friday together.

7. Use the Present Progressive Tense for Current Action

Thepresentprogressivetenseisforanythingthatishappeningrightnow.Allof theprogressivetensesareeasytospotbecausetheirverbsalwaysendwith"-ing" andgetahelpingverb.Ahelpingverbisjustsoweknowwhoandwhenwe`re talkingabout.Inthepresentprogressive,thehelpingverbsarethepresenttense conjugations of "to be."

- I am drinking ice flavored tea.
- The barking dogs outside are driving me mad.
- Paul is playing with his hyper dog.

8. Add "ed" to verbs for the Past Tense

Whenwetalkaboutthepast,wehavetoaddan"-ed"toregularverbstomake thesecondform.Irregularverbsaretrickyandhavetheirownsetsofrules. Drink,forexample,turnsto"drank."Mostofthetime,though,"-ed"willdo.

I drank a lot of choclate flavored coffee yesterday, but Paul didn`t. The dogs stopped barking two seconds ago, and I am feeling relived. Paul played frisbee with his neighbour.

Working with the Perfect Tense

Practicemakesperfectwiththeperfecttenses.Herearethreerulestofinishthe 11rulesofgrammar.Ifyourememberthese,you`llbewellonyourwaytoper- fection.

9. Use Present Perfect for the Unfinished Past

The present perfect can be confusing for some, but it is one of the most important rules of grammar. When people talk about things that have already happened but consider the time in which they occurred to be unfinished, they use the third form of the verb with a helping verb. The helping verb for the present perfect is the present tense conjugation of "to have."

- I have drunk three cups of coffee today.
- Paul`s hyper cur dog has bitten me three times so far.
- Paul has walked his hyper labrador 50 times this week.
- Unfortunately, the only way to know the third forms of verbs is through memory.

10. Use Present Perfect Progressive for Unfinished Action and Past

When the action as well as the time is considered unfinished, the verb loads upon third form helping verbs ("to be" and "to have") and changes to the progressive form.

- Western countries have been waging wars in the East for thousands of years.
- I have been drinking coffee all day.
- Paul`s dog has been barking like crazy since it was born.

11. Use Past Perfect for the First of Two Past Actions

When two things happen in the past, we have to mark which one happened first. The one that happened first changes to third form and gets the helping verb, "had."

- By the time I drank one cup of coffee, Paul`s dog had barked a thousand times.
- I had not yet eaten dinner when Paul walked her dog.
- She could not pay for coffee because she had lost her wallet.

Understanding and consistently following the basic English grammar rules will help you speak and write English correctly and with minimal hesitation.

Notes/Practice Area:

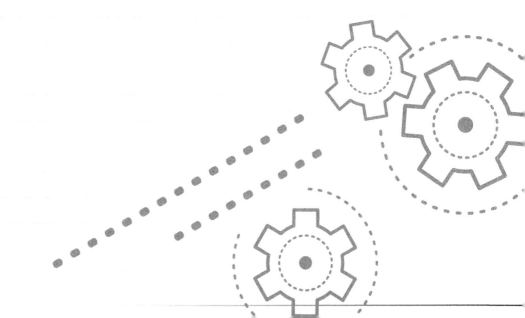

The best birthday party ever would be...

Yesterday I went to the zoo. I saw...

If there were a monster in my closet I would…

If you could be a grown up for a day, what would you do?

VOCABULARY BUILDER 6TH GRADER

Forthisexercise,youarerequiredtoresearchthefollowingwords, discoverthemeaningofeachwordandultimately,usethewordin yourwriting.Onceyouhaveusedeachwordthreetimes,crossthe word from your list. This is a great exercise to repeat later.

adjacent	prediction	factor	consequence
dimension	appropriate	repetition	hypothesis
obedient	exaggerate	citizen	suspense
accumulate	priority	ferocious	construct
drastic	artifact	retrieve	insists
oblivious	exhaust	civilization	tentative
adapt	quote	frequent	continuous
elaborate	benefit	frequency	irrigate
origin	expression	compose	thesis
adequate	realistic	genuine	contrast
encourage	calculate	solution	lofty
peculiar	extend	conclusion	transfer
analyze	recount	government	contribute
equation	catastrophe	strategy	manipulate
persuade	extensive	congruent	unanimous
anticipate	reinforce	history	declare
evaluate	chronological	substitute	massive

^i æ^_ʕq + ✦ pnbb`e    `l ks bop ^qf l k

Notes:

If you could be an animal for a day, what animal would you choose? What would you do?

Write about going back to school after summer vacation.

Write a thank you note to an imaginary friend who gave you onion and garlic-flavored chewing gum.

Finish this thought: if I could change one thing about myself, it would be...

Draw an imaginary constellation. Write a story such as ancient people might have told about it.

Describe a made-up dream or nightmare.

Five years from now, I will be...

Write about a day you'd like to forget.

Write about your favorite childhood toy.

Write out the best day of your life.

Write out the worst day of your life.

When I am a parent, I'll never...

I have never been more frightened than when...

VOCABULARY BUILDER 7TH GRADER

Forthisexercise,youarerequiredtoresearchthefollowingwords, discoverthemeaningofeachwordandultimately,usethewordin yourwriting.Onceyouhaveusedeachwordthreetimes,crossthe word from your list. This is a great exercise to repeat later.

abdicate	mitigate	devastate	estimate
connotation	adequate	omit	prominent
legendary	correspond	alternative	belligerent
abrasive	naive	devious	evaluate
consecutive	admonish	opposition	prospective
liasion	dawdle	amendment	bewilder
abruptly	narrate	devour qpes	bewildered
irrelevant	affiliation	antagonize	exonerated
libel	deceitful	diversity	punctual
acknowledge	necessity	perceive	exposition
consult	agitate	attribute	quote
ludicrous	demeanor	eligible	bias
acquire	negligent	persuasive	exuberant
contrast	allege	authentic	relinquish
mandatory	derogatory	emphasize	boycott fam-
addict	obnoxious	prediction	ished resolve
copious	allocate	bamboozle	condor

^i me^ _bʻq + + pnbb`e ★

`l ks bop ^qf l k

formidable	chronological	tentative	viewpoint
rudimentary	industrious	component	condemn
cause	suspense	inhabitants	irate
impartial	compel	toxic	confront
signify	inevitable	conclusive	
characterize	talisman	initiate trea-	
indifferent	competent	son	
sovereign	infuriate	intimidate	

Notes:

Invent and describe a new food.

Describe an event that changed your life forever, or make up and
describe an event that would change your life forever.

If I were the president, I would...

If I were the principal, I would...

Describe someone who is a hero to you and explain why.

Write about a time in your life when you struggled with a choice and made the right one.

Imagine yourself in a different century and describe an average day in your life.

What would you do if you could travel into the future?

Which character from a book would you most like to meet and why?

Three goals I have set for myself are...

What would you do if someone just gave you $1 million?

What would you do if all the electricity in the world just stopped?

VOCABULARY BUILDER 8TH GRADER

Forthisexercise,youarerequiredtoresearchthefollowingwords,
discoverthemeaningofeachwordandultimately,usethewordin
yourwriting.Onceyouhaveusedeachwordthreetimes,crossthe
word from your list. This is a great exercise to repeat later.

construct	anonymous	rebuke	gruesome
precise	despondent	audacious	similar
abrasive	prudent	evoke	bizarre
contrast	anthology	recur	imminent
prediction	elapse	authority	simulate
alternative	pseudonym	feasible	boycott
corroborate	apathy	resilient	impel
prevalent	embark	avid	simultaneous
ambiguous	quote	focus	capable
depict	apprehend	response	imperative
procedure	encompass	ban	source
amiss	rebel	formula	cause
derive	assimilate	reverberate	integrate
profound	endeavor	belligerent	specific
anarchy	rebuff	generation	characterize
despicable	assumption	significant	interrogate
proprietor	evidence	bisect	spontaneous

^i ɾɛ^_ƀq + + `l ks bop ^qf l k

+ pnbb`e ★

chronological	concise	obsolete	perspective
merge	narrate	variable	consistent
commence	universal	conjecture	persuasive
modify	conclude	opposition	inspire
compels	novice	conscientious	
mutiny	validate	perish	
tirade	confiscate	consecutive	

Notes:

What would you do if 300 mice had just gotten out of their cages in a pet shop where you worked?

What would you do if you were locked inside your favorite department store overnight?

What would you do if you woke up one morning to find yourself completely invisible?

What would you do if you were able to communicate with animals?

What would you do if you could travel into the future?

What would you do if you could travel free anyplace in the world?

What would you do if the dinner served to you in a fancy restaurant came with a fly in the mashed potatoes?

Tell about what triggers anger in you or someone else.

Invent a monster and describe it. Tell where it lives, what it eats, and what it does.

Describe the perfect day. Put in as many details as you can. Make it a possible day, not a "dream day."

What event from history would you most like to have witnessed and why?

Who is the person from literature that you would most like to meet and talk to? Why? What would you like to ask?

What commercial on TV do you dislike beyond all others? What about it is particularly annoying to you?

Compile a list of words that describe you as a child. Compile a second list that describes you as you are now. How are these lists the same? How are they different?

Compile a list of inanimate or animate objects to which you might compare yourself metaphorically. (I am a windmill. I change direction or my thoughts whenever someone talks to me...)

VOCABULARY BUILDER 9TH GRADER

Forthisexercise,youarerequiredtoresearchthefollowingwords,
discoverthemeaningofeachwordandultimately,usethewordin
yourwriting.Onceyouhaveusedeachwordthreetimes,crossthe
word from your list. This is a great exercise to repeat later.

absolve	pacify	formulate	deficient
escalate	approximate	proponent	implication
mediate	exposition	contrast	respective
alleviate	perception	generate	demonstrate
evaluate	arbitrary	punitive	imply
mortify	falter	credible	retaliate
alternative	perspective	gist	depict
exacerbate	attribute	rapport	incentive
niche	feasible	cursory	sabotage
ambivalent	pertinent	hypothetical	derive
excerpt	beneficial	rationale	incoherent
obscure	feign	cynic	scrutiny
analyze	ponder	impartial	detract
exemplify	comprehensive	reconcile	indolent
obsolete	fluctuate	dearth	simulate
animosity	prevalent	implausible	devastate
explicit	connotation	redundant	infamous

^i me^_bq   + \ooV +   `l ks bop^qf l k

pnbb`e ★

squander	intercede	diversion	viable
digress	technique	isolate	elude
infuriate	elude	valid	mandatory
succumb	interpret	elation	vulnerable
dilemma	traumatic	jeopardize	testament
innovation	distort	verify	
tangible	intimidate	elicit	
diligent	turmoil	lucrative	

Notes:

What is your favorite kind of weather? Why?

_____

_____

_____

_____

_____

_____

_____

What is the best book you have ever read? Why did you like it? Did reading the book change you in any way? What way?

_____

_____

_____

_____

_____

_____

_____

Write about what you didn't do this weekend.

If you could go back in time anywhere and "anywhen," where/when would you go and why?

What law would you like to see enacted which would help people? How would it help?

Think about an incident that happened to you and exaggerate in the telling. Make it into a tall tale.

If you were ruler of the world, what things would you banish absolutely for all time (rain on weekends, eggplant, and so forth)? Make a list. Use your imagination.

When I grow up I am going to ....

When I have my license I am going to drive to...

Design some gadget, machine, building, or other creation that might enrich the future. What does it look like? What does it do? How does it function? In what ways might it benefit people?

What current fashion in clothing do you particularly like or dislike? Explain your choices.

Be a building you know well. Talk about your life and memories.

Write about the funniest thing that ever happened to you.

Convince someone why music or art or computers are important in your life. Make them appreciate your viewpoint.

If you had $100,000, how would you spend it?

What if the use of robots in school becomes a workable reality?

What would you pack in your suitcase if you could not go home again?

You are to tell a person from a distant planet or from another era what pollution is. Make that person understand what causes it and why it is bad.

If you could do something that you never have done before, what would it be? Why would you want to do it?

Begin a list of questions that you'd like to have answered. They may be about the future or the past.

What do you consider your greatest accomplishment to date and why?

Write one characteristic or habit about yourself that you like and describe it. Or write about one thing you don't like about yourself.

What is your hobby? Why do you enjoy it?

If you could go somewhere where you've never gone before, where would you go and why?

What's, if anything, would you be willing to fight or even die for?
Explain your answer.

Did your mom or dad ever make you wear something you hated?

If you could change one thing about the world, what would it be?
Why would you make this change?

Is there a machine you feel you could not live without? Explain.

Did you ever stick up for someone?

Describe your neighborhood bully.

Did you ever win or lose a contest? Tell the story about what happened.

Write about a time when you were talked into something and you regretted it.

Write about a baby-sitting experience.

Describe a great fort you built for a great game you played as a child.

Did you ever get lost in a strange town or place?

Were you ever locked in or out? What did you do?

Write about an enemy who eventually became your friend.

Write about a time you cheated and got caught. What did you learn from the experience?

Write about a privilege you earned.

Write about learning to skate, to ride a bike, to climb a tree, or to turn a cart wheel.

Write about the stray animal you brought home.

Did you ever send away for or order something that turned out to be a disappointment?

What is it like to go shopping with your mother or father?

Write about a time you performed in front of an audience.

Write about a difficult decision you had to make.

What was it like to spend your first night away from home?

What was it like to come back home after a long vacation?

Write about a disappointment.

Write about something minor that turned into a big deal.

Were you ever in a helicopter? Tell about it. If not, tell what you think it would be like to be in one.

Were you ever in a limousine? Tell about it. If not, tell what you think it would be like to be in one.

Were you ever in a race car? Tell about it. If not, tell what you think it would be like to be in one.

Were you ever in a hot-air balloon? Tell about it. If not, tell what you think it would be like to be in one.

Were you ever in a horse-drawn carriage? Tell about it. If not, tell what you think it would be like to be in one.

Were you ever in a submarine? Tell about it. If not, tell what you think it would be like to be in one. Describe the sounds, smells etc.

Write about a time you helped someone.

Did you ever forget something really important? What happened as a result?

Write about an experience in a hospital.

Write about a time someone helped you.

What does it mean to be a friend?

Write about your best friend.

Were you ever accused of something that you didn't do?

Describe a favorite outdoor game.

Describe your favorite indoor game.

Write about a time you had a bicycle accident.

Write about a time you went shopping for new clothes.

Write about a time you went shopping for a new toy.

Write about a time your parents embarrassed you.

Write about your favorite birthday memory.

If you had to escort a visitor from outer space for a 30-minute tour of your community, where would you begin and end?

Be a grape that becomes a raisin: describe how it feels to shrink, to shrivel, to become dry and wrinkled.

Be an icicle that becomes water. Describe how it feels to be cold and firm and full of beautiful crystals but only to melt and lose your shape.

I really hate it when my mother/father/sibling...

You go to the store with your parents and baby brother. Your parents go into a store and tell you to watch your brother. You take your eyes off your brother for just a minute and you can't find him. You...

You have just met an alien from another planet. He wishes to take a student back to his planet. Convince him you would be the perfect specimen for him to take.

If you could change one law, what law would it be and how would you change it?

It started out as an unusual Monday morning, when I...

Describe what you think of as the typical mother.

Describe what you think of as the typical father.

As I approached the deserted house at the end of the road, I saw...

Would you rather have a brother or sister? Why

Describe a fight you had with your mother. Now tell it from her point
of view.

Write a short biography of your mother.

Write a short biography of your father.

Visualize a time when your mother was laughing. Recall a time when you two shared a good laugh over something.

Write a physical description of your mother. Write as if you were looking at a movie rather than a photograph.

If you had three wishes, what would they be? (You can not ask for three more wishes)

Concentrate on a particular habit that your mother has and write about it.

What is something special and/or different about you? Why do you think it is special or different?

Imagine yourself as a teacher. What type of student would you like to teach and why?

Write about two things that your family has taught you.

Write about some of the things that you worry about.

Describe a happy memory of your family.

How do you know someone loves you, even if he or she doesn't say it?

Name one thing you like about yourself and why you like it.

If you could be a character in any book, TV show, or movie, who would you be and why?

If you had to work in any store at your favorite mall, which store would it be and why?

What makes you proud of your nationality?

Describe the one thing that gives you the most comfort.

Describe the most difficult thing about being your age.

Describe one possession that means the most to you.

Who is the most important role model in your life?

Who should be paid more, professional athletes or teachers? Why or why not?

Describe your best personality trait.

If you could study one subject in school that wasn't offered, what would it be and why?

What class do you enjoy the most and why?

Write about the worst fight you ever had with a friend.

If you had a chance to live anywhere you could, where would it be and why?

Write about the pros/cons of year-round school or a four-day school week.

Write about your favorite sport.

Is the school year too long? Too short? Why?

What does your summer usually consist of?

Describe your dream house.

If you had only one month to live, what would you do?

Who is your favorite person to be with? Why?

What would be your ideal job when you grow up? Explain.

Describe how you would manage your own radio or TV station.

What is your definition of success?

What do you think your life will be like in 10 years? 20 years?

If you could guest star on any TV show, what would it be and why?

The saying goes, "Money cannot buy happiness." Do you agree or disagree? Why?

How do you imagine life as an adult?

Write about a ship or other vehicle that can take you somewhere different from where you are now.

Write about a rocket-ship on its way to the moon or a distant galaxy far, far, away.

Envision a dragon. Do you battle him? Or is the dragon friendly? Use descriptive language.

Write a story about a conversation you overheard.

Look outside the window. Write a story about what you see.

Write about numbers that mean something to you.

Write a story or poem that starts with the word "hello".

Write about going to the doctor.

Write about going to the dentist.

Write about doing something you don't want to do.

What is something you fear? How can you overcome that fear?

Write about a time you were surprised.

Write about a time you were scared.

Write a story about your grandparent.

Write a letter to a famous person.

If I found $2000 I would...

Write about your favorite teacher.

Make up your own sport. What is it called? How many people can play? What are the rules? How do you play?

Write about someone you miss.

Write about the sounds you hear.

Write about your morning routine.

Write about a place you have never been. Do you want to go there?
Why or why not?

What would happen if kids ruled the world?

Doug stuck his hand in the box and immediately pulled it out. "Ow," he said. He licked the side of his index finger as if it had honey on it. (Continue to write about who Doug is, where he is, and what is in the box...)

A ship carrying animals to a zoo in Argentina is blown off course. A giraffe and a chimpanzee, the only survivors, find themselves shipwrecked in Antarctica. Write a story about a friendship that forms between these two animals and the penguin that comes to their aid.

Make a list of five things that make it hard for you to sleep at night (lumpy pillows, scary movies before bedtime, etc.). Now, make a list of five things that help you fall asleep easily.

Write a paragraph titled "How to Draw a Tomato." Explain the complete process, from gathering supplies to displaying the finished artwork.

The Postal Service has announced a contest for the best camouflage on a front yard mailbox. Describe your prize-winning plan to disguise your family's mailbox.

You're going on a week-long camping trip but you can only take three items. What items would you take, and why?

If you could be any animal you like (real or fantasy), which would you choose, and why?

I have never been more frightened than when...

Imagine someone has asked you to convert the kitchen pantry into either a doll house or a bunker for plastic army men. Explain how would you furnish and decorate this new play space.

A local bakery has invited you to invent a new bagel flavor. Describe your doughy creation using the senses of sight, touch, taste, and smell.

Everyone in your family has a super power. Which family member has which super power and how does each one work?

Imagine that you are an inventor, you invent something that will change the lives of kids all over the world. What would that invention be?

You're stranded on a deserted island with one other person. Who would you hope it was and why?

What would you do if you woke up one morning to find you had x-ray vision and could see everything. Describe what you would see.

Write a list of at least 20 sounds that you like and why.

Describe a routine in your life you enjoy? This can be a routine for bed or getting ready to play a game or going to school on Monday.

If you could travel back in time to any moment, what would it be, and why? Would you change history or just observe?

What is the best birthday present you ever received? What made it so special?

What would happen if you woke up and you had grown to eight feet tall overnight? How would this change your life?

What if everyone lived in space? How would we travel from place to place? What sort of houses would we live in? What would we eat?

Write about a secret adventure you and a friend have completed.

Name one appliance in your home and tell me why you can't live without it.

Explain how bad situations can have a good side.

The thing I wish other people would understand about me is...

Describe several ways a person your age can earn money.

Would you want to visit the moon? Why or why not?

You wake up one morning and discover everybody in your town has been frozen in time for 24 hours, what would you do?

Imagine you woke up and saw a dinosaur in your backyard. Write a story telling what you see and do.

Imagine you opened your own restaurant. Tell the name of your restaurant. Explain what the restaurant looks like, who works there, and what you serve.

Describe your favorite character from a book, a movie, or television.

If you could have any animal for a pet, what would it be? Describe the pet and how you would take care of it.

Write a story titled, "My Journey on a Pirate Ship." You and your friends can star in the story.

Do you have any brothers or sisters? If you do, tell what they're like.
If not, tell whether or not you would like to have a brother or sister.

If you could have lunch with any famous person who would it be? What would you talk about with this person?

Write a story titled, "The Bat Who Couldn't Fly."

Imagine you were a wonderful painter and your parents would let
you paint anything you wanted on your bedroom walls. What would you
paint? Use lots of details to describe your artwork.

Describe the oldest person you know.

Describe the youngest person you know.

Do you think a monkey would make a good pet? Explain why or why not.

How old were you four years ago? Describe some things you can do now that you could not do then.

Write a story titled, "The Baby Dragon."

Imagine you worked at a football stadium. What would your job be? (examples: quarterback, cheerleader, coach, referee, ticket seller) Describe what you would do while you were on the job.

What do you like best about your home?

If you could be on any game show, what would it be? Describe what happens when you're on the show.

Describe your favorite season (fall, spring, summer, or winter). Tell what kinds of things you like to do during that season.

If you could spend an afternoon with one member of your extended family, who would it be? Tell why you chose this person and tell what you do together.

Which superpower would you most like to have-- invisibility, super strength, or the ability to fly? Describe what kinds of things you would do with your powers.

Think of a time when you've won something. Tell what you won and how you won it.

Invent a new kind of sandwich. Describe what is on it and how you would make it.

Describe one thing you're really good at and how it makes you feel.

Imagine you were twenty feet tall. Describe what life would be like.

If you were a doctor, what kind of doctor would you be? (examples: children's doctor, veterinarian, eye doctor, dentist) Tell what your job would be like.

Write about your first day of school.

Write a story about the day you were born.

What do you like best about your school?

Pretend you had $100, but you weren't allowed to keep it for yourself. You have to give it away to a charity or person. Who would you give the money to? What would you want the person to do with it?

Write about someone you know who has shown perseverance.

Describe one time when you were brave.

Who is the bravest person you know? Why?

Who is the kindest person you know? Why?

If you could cook any meal for your family, what would you cook?
Describe the meal and tell how you would make it.

Imagine you have climbed the highest tree in your neighborhood,
describe what you can see.

What talent would you most like to have in the future and why?

Imagine you woke up and saw a bear in your kitchen. Write a story telling what you see and do.

What is your favorite thing to write?

I love it when my mom...

I love it when my dad...

Who has the best job in the world?

Where do you get your best ideas?

Imagine that you are stuck inside a TV. What will you do? What shows would you visit?

What would you do if you won the lottery?

Would you rather be an animal or a toy?

Write a poem about school.

If it rained food, what would you want the forecast to look like?

What is your favorite road trip game?

Do you prefer popsicles or ice cream cones? Why?

If you could read minds, whose mind would you read? What do you think you will discover?

Would you ever change your name? What would be your new name?

Write a story about someone who tells bad jokes.

Write a story in which you are a mini marshmallow in a cup of hot chocolate.

Write an alternate ending to your favorite book.

What is the best kind of breakfast food? Why?

Write about your favorite sports team. Why?

Why does the government provide public education?

Do you like your first name? Does it fit your personality?

Write a poem about fall.

What is your favorite memory as a kid growing up?

Make a list of all the things you've accomplished this week. How do you feel?

If you were a professional singer, what genre of music would you sing?

What is your favorite milkshake flavor and why?

What is the best sound in the world and why?

What is the best sight in the world and why?

If you could be a dinosaur for a day, which kind would you be and what would you do for the day?

What is your favorite thing to do outside and why?

Have you ever had a scary dream and laughed about it later? Describe the dream and how you felt at the time.

Write about a memory that makes you happy.

How can you give back to your community?

What would it be like to live on the moon?

How does it feel to miss someone or something?

What is life all about?

If you could visit any single new city in the world, where would you go?

Your shoe must have a story to tell. Tell it.

Describe your favorite character from a book, a movie, or television.

What would happen if you encountered a talking squirrel? Describe
the experience.

Write a story about trading places with your favorite TV, movie, or rock star.

Write about the best party you've ever been to.

One day a spaceship lands on the playground of your school...

Your class grew plants as a science project. One day you looked at your plant and saw something really strange had grown there.

Write a story about what it would be like if you woke up one morning with wings.

On your birthday, a strange-looking lady came to you door and handed you a wrapped present. You rattled it. It made a noise. Write a story about this present.

Your teacher one day announced that your class was going on a wonderful field trip. Write a story about this field trip. In your story, you can have your class go anywhere you wish.

One day, as you were petting and talking to your friend's dog, it answered back! Write a story about this.

Write a story about yourself as a hero. What did you do to become a hero? Tell your story.

As you walked down the hallway at school, you heard some strange
music coming from the custodian's closet. What was it? Write a story
about it.

Tell a story about children who live in a world where there is no such thing as television, computers, or electronic games.

A distant relative bequeathed you a strange ring. As you put this ring on, you discover that it has strange powers. What does it look like? What does it do? Tell a story about this ring.

Tell a story about your ideal place to live. What would it be like to live here?

The teacher comes into the room and places a bag on her desk then leaves. The bag moves and wriggles. Write a story about what is in the paper bag.

Everyone has a day in his or her life that was extra special or dreams about what he or she would do on a special day. Write a story about a special day you have had or imagine you might have.

Every day you pass a door. It's always closed and locked. One day, as you pass, you notice that the door is open. You step inside. Write a story about what was on the other side of that door.

Tell a story about what happened when you traveled on a wagon pulled by horses.

Tell a story about a day in which everything went wrong.

Imagine you could travel to the future and live there. Think of what you think the future would be like. How different would it be from today? Now, write a story about living in the future.

Imagine you could go to any place you wanted for as long as you wanted any time you wanted. What place would you visit? Think about what you would do there. Write a story about a visit to a really neat place.

Pretend that you lived in colonial times. Think about what your life would be like, how it would be different living more than 200 years ago. Now, write a story about a young person (or yourself) living in George Washington's day.

Novels are fun to read because the action keeps you interested, and the characters almost become your friends. Think of a book you really liked. Imagine that you were a new character in this book (choose a book your class has read). Write a story about what happened.

Imagine you woke up one morning and found that you had switched places with a dog or a cat. Think what it would be like. What would you do? Write a story of your day as a dog or a cat.

What if you had a personal genie who would grant your every wish? What would your life be like? Think of some of the details. Write a story about having a personal genie.

Imagine you had a car that would take you anywhere you wanted to go for one day. Think of where you went in that car and what you did. Write a story about that day.

Everyone has a favorite season of the year. What is your favorite season? What do you like to do? Write a story about your favorite season.

One spring day a skunk wanders into your classroom. What are the results? Write a story about the skunk that visited school.

Imagine a world where there was no money. What would people do? What would life be like? Write a story about living in a world without any money.

Imagine one morning there's a knock at your front door. You open the door, and to your great surprise, you find an alien standing there. What do you do? What does it look like? Write story about your encounter with this alien.

On your way to school one morning you see a huge truck speeding down the road. Suddenly, the back door of the truck opens and a large, mysterious box falls off the back of the truck. It sits there in the road. What is in the box? What do you do? Write a story about this mysterious box.

Imagine you had a time machine that you could take only to the past. Where would you choose to go? Think of what you would do there, what it would the like, who would you take with you? Write a story of your adventure in the past.

One day you are sitting under a large tree. An acorn hits you on the head, and you look up. There, on the branch above you sits a squirrel, laughing at you. The squirrel then looks you square in the eye, begins to talk to you, and asks you to return its acorn. What would you do?

There are times when we all wish, even for just a moment, that we could be someone else for a day. Who would you choose to be for that day? What would you do? Think of some details of your day. Now write a story about what your day was like as that person.

In a recent disaster, there were some kids who did some heroic things. Think what constitutes (makes) a hero. Imagine yourself as one. Now write a story in which you were a hero/heroine in a tough situation.

A little old lady gave you and a friend some magical glitter and told you to sprinkle it on your hair and something special would happen. What happened when you tried it? Write a story about this mysterious magical glitter.

One day you and your friends walked up to an old, seemingly abandoned house. You couldn't see inside due to the dust and cobwebs on the windows. You decide to see if the door is locked. You try the knob, and it turns. The door creaks open as if it has not opened in years. What happens next? What do you find? What do you and your friend do? Write a story about entering that old, seemingly abandoned house.

Love comes in all forms. We can love our parents, a boyfriend or girlfriend, a favorite pet, a brother or sister, a place, even a thing. Thing about someone or something you love. Write a story about that person or thing that involves your feelings.

Imagine that your sense of smell was more highly developed than everyone else's. What experiences might you have? How might your life change? What would you be able to smell? Write a story about a person with a very highly developed sense of smell.

Imagine yourself temporarily lost in a foreign country where you do not know the language. How do you manage to communicate? What might happen to you? Write a story about a day you might have spent lost in a foreign country without knowing the language.

Imagine a city project to have every school student do some hours of community service as a part of the required curriculum. What would you choose to do? What do you think it would be like? What people might you meet? What would you be doing to help? Write a story about your day of community service.

Sometimes family members or friends embarrass you when other people are around. Think of sometimes this has happened to you. Think of what could happen. Write a story about some embarrassing incident you might have had and how you coped with it.

Sign Up to ThomasMedia.ie

Thomas Media is an independent publisher based in Dublin, Ireland. At Thomas Media, we are passionate about books and our readers. We would like to invite you to become a member of community and enjoy exclusive benefits. With already 25,000 happy customers worldwide, we promise you'll be in good company.

Up to 50% off your next website purchases

Access to free offers

Birthday gifts

Free shipping offers

First dibs on sales

& more...

To subscribe, simply visit our website at:

http://www.thomasmedia.ie/subscribe.html

365 Creative Series

365 Creative Series

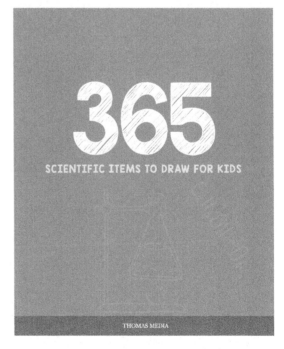